Sally
and the constellations

For
Merryn and
Patton!

Written by **Anna Courie**

Illustrated by **Karen Deming**

For some time now, Sally the Comet had been flying through space meeting the different planets. She loved that she had friends

Fun Fact
Mercury, Venus, and Earth are the three planets closest to the Sun.

all over the solar system, but she noticed that the planets were busy doing things in their own orbits.

Sally was bored.

Sally decided to go see the Sun.

"Hello, Sun! It is me, Sally the Comet!
I came to visit," she said.

Fun Fact

Comets orbit the
solar system at
different speeds and
distances which is
why we see them
at different
times.

"Hello, Sally!"
said the Sun. "It has
been a long time
since I've seen you.

Your travels have been
very long. Did you make
friends with the planets?"

"Oh yes!" she said. "I met all the planets. The planets are now my friends, even Pluto. I still think of Pluto as a planet, even if the rest of the world does not. They all are fun and unique."

Fun Fact
Sally's favorite planet is Pluto. Sally thinks that Pluto should still be a planet.

The Sun replied, "That is so wonderful! Having friends in many places is a great thing.

You will always have someone to visit
no matter where you are. But I see you
have a sad face. Whatever is wrong?"

"Ohhhhhhhhh, I'm boooooooooooored!"

"All my friends
are busy
in their
own orbits
and I have
nothing to dooooooooooooooo."

Fun Fact
Planets, comets,
and asteroids
all circle the
sun in paths
called "orbits."

"That's rubbish!"
said the Sun.

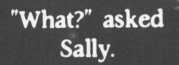

"What?" asked Sally.

"Rubbish! You have the whole universe as your playground.

There are so many things to do and see," replied the Sun. "Have you explored the moons, the asteroids, or even the constellations?"

Fun Fact
The asteroid belt separates the inner, rocky planets and the outer, gaseous planets.

Sally was shocked. She had not thought about anything besides the planets. "What are constellations?" she asked.

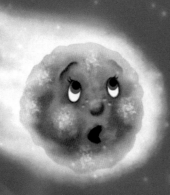

Fun Fact

Constellations are imaginary pictures or shapes that people see in groups of stars.

The Sun said, "I am going to send you on a scavenger hunt in space to find these different constellations, and then you can tell me what they are.

This is what I want for you to find while you fly around: a hunter, a bull, a scorpion, the twins, a horse with wings, and a dragon."

"I don't believe you! I have been flying all around and I have never seen any of those things," Sally told the Sun.

Fun Fact
Stars do not change position in the night sky, so people have used them to navigate while traveling at night.

"If you look to the stars, you will find what I see," said the Sun.

Fun Fact

The Sun is a star which is at the center of our solar system.

"Off you go, little comet."

Sally flew off into space.

She needed to find a hunter. She hoped it was not a Comet Hunter! The Sun told her to look to the stars. "What does the Sun see that I don't see?" she wondered.

Suddenly, certain stars started to stand out in the night sky.

There! She could see shoulders, feet, and a bow cocked with an arrow. A head started to take shape, so Sally decided to connect the dots as she flew from star to star.

Fun Fact

There is no such thing as a comet hunter. Sally is being silly.

As Sally connected the dots, the hunter came to life!
"Who goes there?" the hunter roared.

Fun Fact
Constellations often have names of characters from Greek and Roman mythology (which are ancient stories).

Sally replied,
"Hello, Hunter. I am
Sally the Comet.
Who are you?"

"I am Orion," he said,
"Known as the 'Great Hunter.'
I am made of three famous
stars, Betelgeuse, Rigel,
and Bellatrix.

I am currently hunting
the Bull. Can you
help me find him?"

Fun Fact

The famous
stars, Betelgeuse,
Rigel, and Bellatrix
make up Orion's
shoulders and
left knee.

"Hello, Orion. How exciting to be a hunter. I did not know there was a bull in the sky. I will go look for him for you as well. When I come back on my orbit, I will let you know if I find him."

Fun Fact

The easiest way to find Orion in the night sky is to look for the three stars in a row that make up his belt.

"Thank you, Sally," said Orion. "I look forward to the report on your travels."

So Sally flew off through
space in search of a bull.
She peered into space again
and let her imagination
take over.

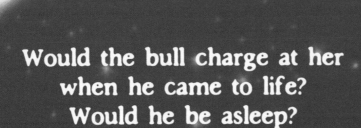

Would the bull charge at her
when he came to life?
Would he be asleep?

Once again certain stars looked like
they were shining brighter than
the others were.

Fun Fact

Taurus, the bull,
is one of twelve
constellations
along an area of
our sky called
the Zodiac.

There! A head. Horns. A tail swishing in the sky.

Fun Fact

The Zodiac are the constellations which lie along the ecliptic, the path that the sun, moon, and planets follow through the sky.

The bull
was
awake.

"Hello, I am
Sally the Comet.
Who are you?"

"I am Taurus, the Great Bull!"
he bellowed. "I will charge you!
I will stomp you, and I will
butt heads with you!"

Fun Fact

The red giant star
Aldebaran is the
brightest star in the
constellation and
is known as the
Eye of Taurus.

"Oh, please don't do that," said Sally.
"I just want to be your friend.

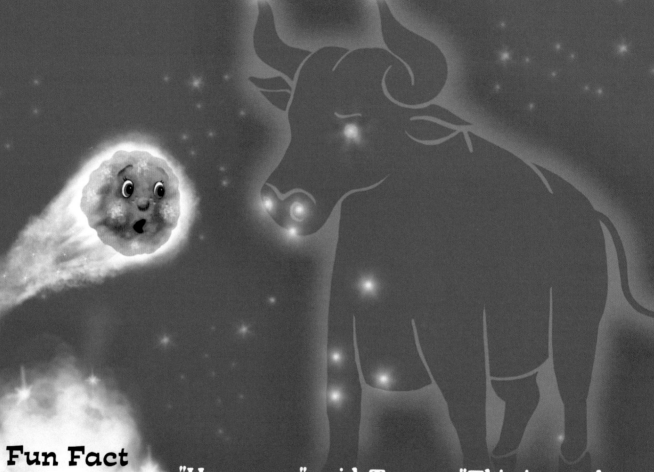

"The hunter, Orion, is looking for you. You might want to be careful. He has a big bow and arrow."

Fun Fact
There are twelve constellations in the Zodiac.

"Hmmmm..." said Taurus. "This is good news to have. A friend looks after a friend. I must hide. I don't want to be found by Orion. Thank you, my friend."

Sally loved using her imagination to see
things in the sky that she had not noticed before.

She realized she
was no longer bored.

Fun Fact
If you were to
draw lines in the
sky to connect the
stars of Taurus,
this is what it
would look like.

As Sally flew, the stars took shape once again.

There was a long tail, a long and mighty neck and

Fun Fact
Stars are massive, hot balls of plasma held together by gravity.

... watch out!

Sally dodged
a stream of fire
as a dragon
took shape.

Fun Fact
Our Sun is a
nearby star, but
all other stars are
so far away that we
only see them as
tiny points of
light.

"I am Draco the dragon!"
he roared. "I am
going to catch you
by your tail!"

Fun Fact
You can see
Draco the dragon
and all of the
constellations in
the night sky.

Before Sally knew it,
Draco was chasing her in the sky.
He kept trying to bite her tail.

Sally did not like this adventure.
She decided she would find a calmer friend.

Sally took off at the speed of light,
leaving Draco in the distance.

As Draco faded away, Sally
once again looked deep
into the stars for more
shapes to appear.

Fun Fact
Draco is circumpolar.
That means, in the
northern latitudes
you can always
find him because
Draco never sets.

As Draco faded away, Sally once again looked deep into the stars for more shapes to appear.

She noticed that two stars stood out. They looked identical. She was having a hard time telling them apart.

As she flew closer, the stars began to take shape. They were human figures.

Fun Fact
The constellation Gemini actually has 85 stars, not just the two brightest stars.

"Hello!" Sally called out. "I am Sally the Comet and I am looking for friends in the night sky."

"Hello Sally. We are Castor and Pollux," they spoke in unison. "We are twins. We are great sailors of Greek fame. Our quest is to find the golden fleece."

Fun Fact

The Golden Fleece was supposed to identify the king of Greece.

"Wow," said Sally. "That sounds dangerous. Perhaps I can freeze my tail into an ice sword and defeat foes with a swish of my tail."

Fun Fact

If Sally's tail was on fire, it would melt! Sally is using her imagination. Comets are made of frozen water, gases, and dust.

Her imagination was taking off. Sally could see herself with a cape, helmet, and a fierce flaming tail!

Suddenly, Sally saw something else in the sky
raising its tail like a sword!

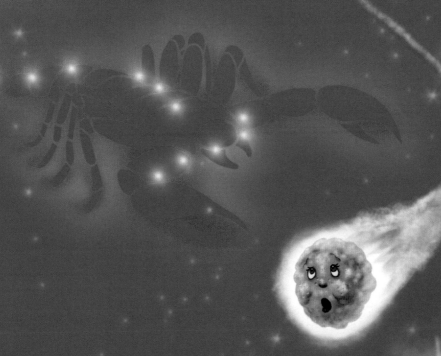

Yikes! A scorpion took shape
amongst the stars and it
was coming right for Sally.

"I am Scorpio," the beast roared!

Fun Fact

The ancient Greeks
believed Scorpio
killed Orion.

The scorpion was attacking Sally! Scorpio did not look like the kind of friend Sally wanted to make.

Sally knew from her travels that friends do not hurt each other; they take care of each other. She also knew that no amount of fun was worth getting hurt.

Fun Fact

Scorpions are real animals with eight legs, two claws, and a stinger. They live in hot climates like deserts.

As Sally calmed down, she remembered that she had to find one more constellation for the Sun.

She thought hard. She remembered the Sun telling her that she needed to find a horse with wings.

"A horse with wings?" she thought. How ridiculous! Surely, the Sun was teasing her.

Fun Fact

You can see the horse with wings in the summer night's sky!

As she flew, she searched the stars eagerly for new shapes. Finally, there it was: a horse with wings!

"Hello, horse! My name is Sally the comet, and I am on an adventure to find new friends in the stars."

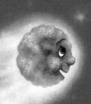

Fun Fact

The ancient Greeks made up many stories to explain the world around them. These stories make up Greek mythology.

"Hello, Sally," said the horse. "I am Pegasus. I am an adventurer too. My rider is Perseus, son of Zeus, and I carry his lightning bolts in the sky. Would you like to take a ride through the sky on me?"

So Sally climbed on Pegasus' back. She pretended her tail was a lightning bolt and that she and Pegasus were off on an adventure to fight evil creatures.

No one could catch them since Pegasus could fly so fast!

Fun Fact

The constellation Pegasus has galaxies in it!

As Pegasus and Sally finished their adventure, she realized she was back by the Sun.

Pegasus flew off and Sally went to tell the Sun how much she enjoyed the scavenger hunt.

"Hello, Sun," called Sally. "Thank you for my amazing adventure.

Fun Fact
The Sun is 92.96 million miles from Earth.

I found Orion the hunter, Taurus the bull, Castor and Pollux the twins, Draco the dragon, Scorpio the scorpion, and Pegasus the winged horse!"

"Well done, Sally," said the Sun. "What else did you learn on this adventure?"

Fun Fact

There are many more constellations in the sky to learn about!

"Sun, I learned that my imagination can take
me to amazing places. My imagination lets me dream
of great things."

The Sun replied, "Yes Sally, when you use your
imagination, you will never be bored."

Sally flew off for more adventures. In her mind, she had on her cape, a flaming lightning bolt sword, and a helmet of gold in which to slay dragons, discover treasure, and explore the solar system with her imagination.

In her mind, Sally was happy.

Fun Fact

Before television, movies, and computers, people had to rely on their imagination to tell stories.